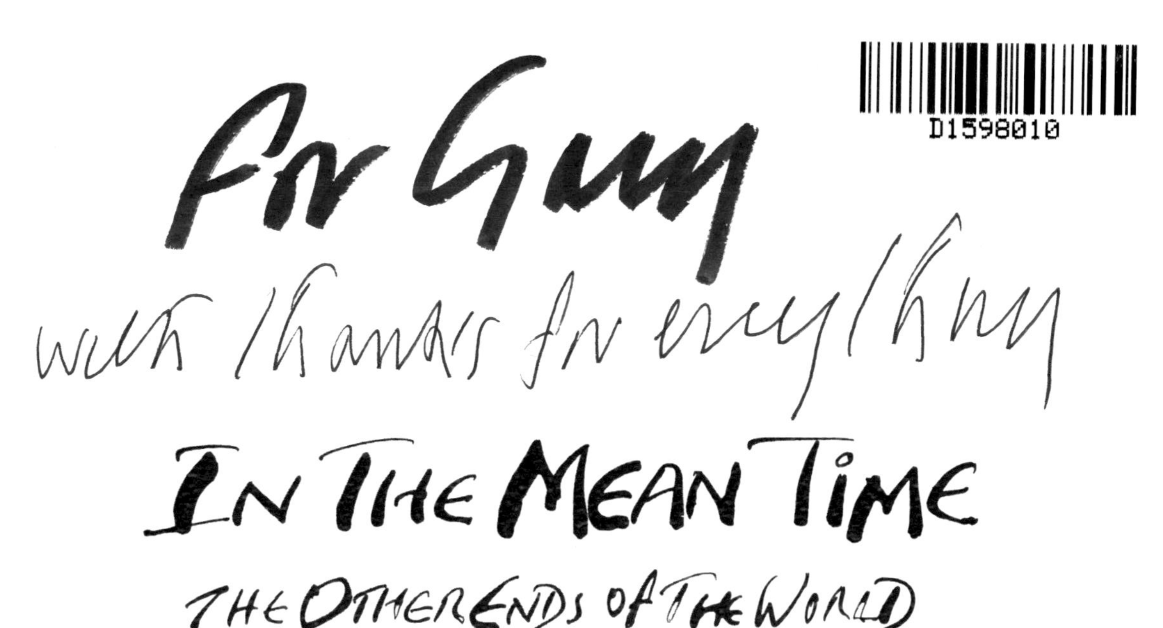

For Guy
with thanks for everything

IN THE MEAN TIME

THE OTHER ENDS OF THE WORLD

CARTOONS & DARK LIGHT VERSE

ANTHONY HADEN-GUEST

PUBLISHED BY

Freight + Volume / Volume Editions 2010

PUBLISHER
Nick Lawrence

ART DIRECTION + DESIGN
Emily Anderson

EDITOR
Yasha Wallin

VISIT US

530 West 24th Street, New York, NY 10011
www.freightandvolume.com / info@freightandvolume.com
212.691.7700

SPECIAL THANKS

to everyone who worked so hard and so bravely to make this happen.

PRINTED BY

Apex Printing, Atlanta, GA in an edition of 2500 paperback.
Additionally there are 30 signed, limited edition hardcovers (26 lettered A–Z, with two artist's proofs, and two publisher's proofs) all with an original drawing by the artist.

TABLE OF CONTENTS

PUBLISHER'S PREFACE

My first encounter with Anthony Haden-Guest's cartoons was also my first encounter with the man himself. A sizable group of gallerists, artists and friends were gathered around a long table at London's Nobu, vigorously celebrating opening night at Frieze in a boom year. Suddenly, the older fellow seated across from me – whom I had previously written off since he was passed out over a plate of sea urchin linguini – awoke and began furiously scribbling a sketch of me and my companion in black ink directly on the tablecloth, all the while punctuating his efforts with repeated punches in the air. The fruits of his labor were soon revealed – a sly drawing captioned "The Art World Takes Shape" – which Anthony immediately and cleverly severed from the rest of the tablecloth, unbeknownst to the restaurant staff, and gave to me. Soon after Anthony was again snoozing into a dessert plate of green tea millefuille, but an indelible friendship had been born – etched in the cloth and my heart. Many moons and adventures with him later, that scrap of cloth is now framed and hanging in my office along with some of his other efforts – some less flattering such as his wily portrait of a gallery owner (*moi?*) with a cell phone entitled "No Connection" – but never without affection.

Thurberesque in their style and simplicity, Dorothy Parkeresque in their wicked humor and sarcasm, Anthony's sketches are not merely cartoons – but bona fide works of art, performance pieces in themselves, adventures in the art trade – which I've been delighted to present at many subsequent fairs. It is a great treat to see such a large number of his drawings finally assembled – scraps of paper, cloth, envelopes et al – in one place. And it's an honor to present *In The Mean Time* to the public – as much as it's been a pleasure to know the man over the years. Should you, as I did, suddenly find yourself the unwitting target of Anthony's biting pen – accept the "punishment" with grace and a large dollop of salt – and you will be amply rewarded.

Nick Lawrence
Freight + Volume

OF COURSE, REALLY
I SHOULD BE GETTING
PAID FOR THIS

INTRODUCTION

The drawings and writings you see here were mostly done fairly recently but come out of how I have been working for many years. Each practice has had a different trajectory in my life, though. I began publishing cartoons as a student at Cambridge, where I was greatly impressed by the eye for character in the work of the late Mark Boxer. I drew regularly for *The Sunday Telegraph* and after I moved to Manhattan for *New York Magazine*, then *The New York Observer*. And now sporadically for magazines, newspapers, online and many, many napkins.

It was also in Manhattan that I began showing in galleries from time to time, as well a couple of stores. But it was only when I started to hand-write the words on my drawings a few years ago, incorporating them fully into the pieces, that I began to feel they were sometimes working the way I meant them to. Was this as "art"? Whatever. Just as long as it didn't swamp the joke.

It is, I think, no accident that *In The Mean Time* has been put together by an art gallerist. There isn't much of an editorial cartoon sensibility to be seen in the media in Britain or America these days, which I find both sad and puzzling, but working within the context of the art world has increasingly become the default mode at the upper end of the culture.

As to the rhymes, well, I have been writing, publishing and performing these for ages too – In 1970 I gave a reading at the Bob Dylan Isle of Wight Festival but in mid-afternoon, so a time when much of the huge audience could be safely assumed to be somewhat, um, unfocussed. But I was happy as a clam as a magazine writer when being a magazine writer seemed the best writing life imaginable. The verses just came and went. Reporting was the main event.

Then the Internet began its rampage through the media. And then came the recession and a general darkening. Suddenly I had found my subject. Or my subject had found me.

It will be noticed, by the way, that I have avoided using that baggage-loaded word "poetry" to describe my rhymes. John Gay called what he wrote for *The Beggar's Opera* "songs." W.S. Gilbert wrote *Bab Ballads and Savoy Songs*, which he illustrated with his own comic drawings. Edward Lear wrote *Laughable Lyrics* – okay, he wrote *Nonsense Poems* too – for which he made his own proto-surrealist comic drawings. Captain Harry Graham, late of the Coldstream Guards, wrote *Ruthless Rhymes for Heartless Homes*. Hilaire Belloc described *More Peers* as "verses." Noel Coward and Lorenz Hart wrote "lyrics." So there's a glittering cast of writers using rhyme to whack home comical or bittersweet meaning and I am content to be of their company, even if not center-stage.

Anthony Haden-Guest
New York, November 2010

SOME THINGS I KNOW

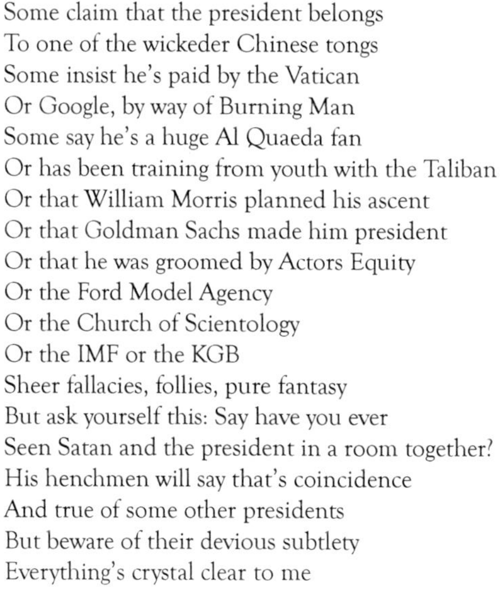

Some claim that the president belongs
To one of the wickeder Chinese tongs
Some insist he's paid by the Vatican
Or Google, by way of Burning Man
Some say he's a huge Al Quaeda fan
Or has been training from youth with the Taliban
Or that William Morris planned his ascent
Or that Goldman Sachs made him president
Or that he was groomed by Actors Equity
Or the Ford Model Agency
Or the Church of Scientology
Or the IMF or the KGB
Sheer fallacies, follies, pure fantasy
But ask yourself this: Say have you ever
Seen Satan and the president in a room together?
His henchmen will say that's coincidence
And true of some other presidents
But beware of their devious subtlety
Everything's crystal clear to me

Some other concerns I'd like to share
You've seen those baldies everywhere?
They're easy to spot since they mostly wear black
They're not ordinary folk who've lost their hair
That's just an innocent, natural lack
But those shiny domes, the superior stare.
All artsy-fartsy, nose in the air.
Twinkly-toed and debonair
Well, they have baldie scientists who know how to train
Your hair to feed messages straight to your brain
Then zap! You're a zombie, a veggie, a pod
On your knees, adoring a baldie god
They are hatching their plans in secrecy
But everything's crystal clear to me

I may not matter too much to you
Being that I'm not smart or famous or rich
But you just may discover before we're through
That I can be one son-of-a-bitch
You see, we're a million-headed man

Each of us thinks a bit differently
But every one of us knows of the plan
To keep us in our place indefinitely
That's their selfish mentality
But we'll know when the time is ripe to make
Our move, get up on our feet and take
Back what what belongs to us. Then we'll break
The shackles of social security
Do away with the NEA
Who are set on turning our children gay
Incarcerate the sex industry
Re-define civil liberty
Oh, there's treats in store for you and me
Everything's crystal clear to me

When aliens from beyond the stars
Thought to check out the human race
They knew they would need a welcoming space
A dive you can find just about any old place
Where they can probe our parts at a leisurely pace
So they're here disguised as Irish bars
Those shamrocks and harps are decoys designed
By an evil galactic mastermind
As I'm sitting here over a Jameson or three
Everything's crystal clear to me

Global warming's a ludicrous lie
Listen up and I'll tell you just why
Would the Good Lord have given us motorcars
Without sure supplies of affordable gas?
No birds in the skies? No fish in the lakes?
Their numbers are lies, their pictures are fakes
Those warmers are in a conspiracy
They're monsters of mendacity
And if I'm a little bit out on this
You're going to burn twice! But I'm heading for bl
Our names are writ in a golden book
A friend of a friend of a friend took a look
The book is in a cavern bored
In the mountains where our nukes are stored
Awaiting the call of an Angry Lord
I have this on the Highest Authority
So everything's crystal clear to me ◘

LAMENT FOR LOST TRADES

In the Beginning was The Word.
Then came The Internet.

I topped every smart kid's wanna-be list
I was a Media Gold Medallist
An investigative journalist
You know who hit the nail on the head?
Rudyard Kipling when he said
Ah! What avails the classic bent
And what the cultured word,
Against the undoctored incident
That actually occurred?
In the weekend colour supplements
I'd sink my teeth into raw events
That was when True and False were king
And a posse of editors rode hard
On every single printed word
And there was an actual job called Fact Checking
But now that our attention span
Is more Neanderthal than Man
There isn't much in the papers and mags
Except recycled celebrity slags,
Their diets, their gardens, their feuds, their shags
Blogs and freesheets, tweets and posts
Have us trapped in a bush of jabbering ghosts

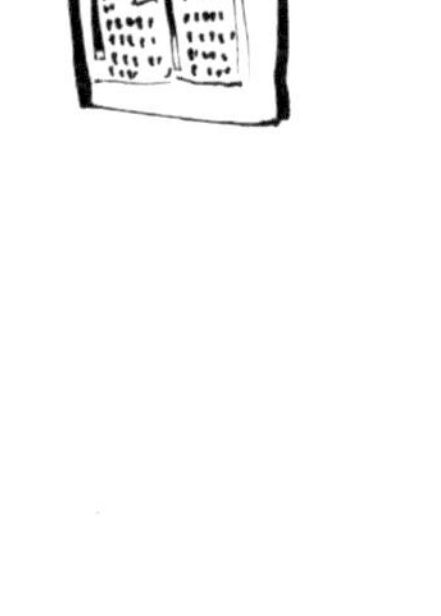

I was a prince and a pasha of porn
In publishing one of the powers that be
My life was the stuff of male reverie
Stars in the pool, peacocks on the lawn,
A ravishing girl in the Jacuzzi,
Waiting so utterly temptingly
As naked as the day she was born,
Inviting as Vegas and pink as a prawn
But now she and the other lovelies have gone
To cyberspace where anyone can see
What I sold being given away for free
Where nobody has to pay to play
And there's nothing on earth as yesterday
As being host of yesterday's fantasy

I'm the butler
I'm the cook
We're the maids!
I'm the chauffeur
The gardener
We're the valets!

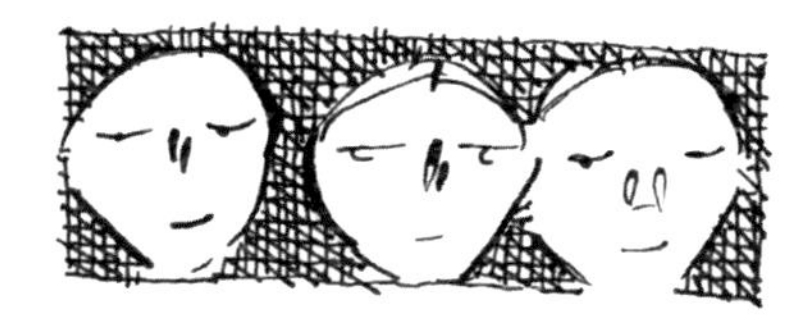

From the hall, the grange, the castle, the palace
But country house lives are not just as they were
M'lady's a thrift shop connoisseur
And take-out is hunky-dory for Sir
S they've sold up their statelies
To Ivan-come-latelies
Whose staffing requirements differ quite greatly
And can cause quite a bit of a countryside stir
There's a food taster and a package inspector
Who also has skills with a metal detector
He knows the vulnerable human spots
And wears a Hugo Boss suit and a Glock
The limos are armored to take quite a knock
And there are missile systems on all of the yachts
As for the old-time staff, well we
Just settle down and watch TV
Where countryside murders are hotter than hot
The Oriental knife on the tennis court
The man-trap in the shrubbery
The headless body in the library
The cyanide in the afternoon tea
And you can dream things are just as they used to be

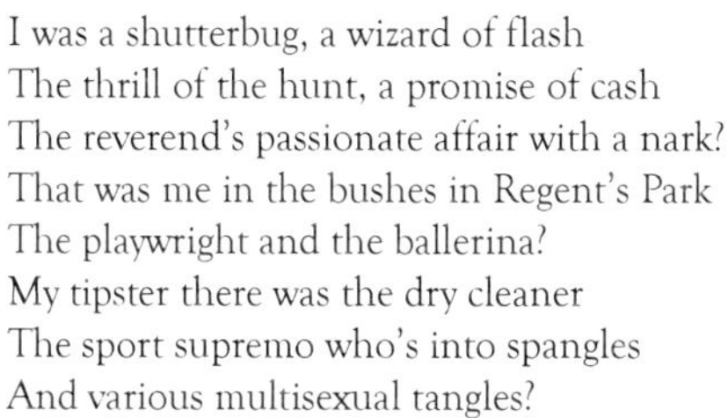

I was a shutterbug, a wizard of flash
The thrill of the hunt, a promise of cash
The reverend's passionate affair with a nark?
That was me in the bushes in Regent's Park
The playwright and the ballerina?
My tipster there was the dry cleaner
The sport supremo who's into spangles
And various multisexual tangles?

I got the greatest camera angles!
But now a swarm of amateurs
Armed with mutant cameras
Are there already on the scene
And gone before I've even been
It was the techies who pulled the plug
Too late, too late, the shutterbug

I was an explorer. I roamed wild places
I trudged through thrilling unmapped spaces.
Teeming jungles, the ocean deep
There was no mountain range too steep
Wooden pitons, a rope, a tent
When the weather cleared up I went
Now fellows who would take a fitness test
At risk of cardiac arrest
Are babied up Mount Everest
Teenage girls get off the phone
And sail around the world alone
Gazillionaires and Champagne Charlies
Toast the Aurora Borealis
As from pole to pole they hop
Watching the whale hunts down below
And dwindling herds drift to and fro
Go to the Amazon to shop
Cross the Sahara in custom cars
Or book rockets to the stars
These are our world's adventurers
But this is not the world that was ◘

GOODBYE TO ALL THIS

Oh what a shame! The world just exploded
Nobody told me it was loaded
Humpty Dumpty took a big fall
Right from the top of the Berlin Wall
Then Wall Street, then any wall at all
So, ladies and gentleman, it's the last call
It's yo-ho-ho! Geronimo!
That's all folks! Got to go!

Goodness gracious! The world is crumbling
All of the dreaming spires are tumbling
The Colosseum, the Golden Gate,
The Tower of Pisa, the Empire State
Angkor Wat, the Parthenon
Frank Gehry's Guggenheims, all gone
Rem Koolhaas and Jean Nouvel
The Birds Nest and the Gherkin blown to hell
Prince Charles is taking this quite well
Whoops!! There goes the Taj Mahal
St Peter's, St Paul's, the Albert Hall
Stonehenge is rubble. It's goodbye to them all

My socks are sizzling, the world is burning
But who gives a shit as long as you're earning?
You'll be a winner in the human race
If you move your arse to cyberspace
A domain of luminous liberty
And wholesale hyperreality
Where everything is completely free
Except for suckers like you and me

Splish! Splash! Splosh! The whole world's drowning
JG Ballard wasn't clowning
So Torremolinos, Tangier, Torquay
Holland, the Hamptons and Waikiki
Are swallowed up by the Dead Sea

Malibu, Montego, Monaco
Sleep with Atlantis down below
Vintage postcards record each scene
See Venice and die in a submarine

Shiver my timbers! The world is freezing
Even A-listers are snuffliing and sneezing
Botox and waxing and looking nice
Getting on Gawker or tabloid TV
Into Heat, Page Six or Ici Paris
Or the club of the moment as a VVIP
Won't mean too much, and this is free advice,
When Mondo Celebrity is sheeting in ice

Hubble, bubble, gubble! The world just melted.
That was unexpected. I really felt it!
The Mona Lisa and Manet and Monet
And Salvador Dali, who was already quite gummy,
And Damien's Shark and the Jeff Koons Bunny
Have all gone gooey and oozey and runny
And not worth a bean in anyone's money

So it's Ta for now! The world just ended
It was broke and it couldn't be mended
And to think that I thought that our trips to space meant
We'd be exchanging our ruined basement
For a brand-new planet, a stunning replacement
With butterflies and bumblebees
And naturally foaming seas
Alpine meadows, coral reefs
Rainforest, downs and windswept heaths
With very few to spoil the view
Just some people I like, perhaps a few of you
But it didn't work out. So it's tootle-oo!

SPEAKING FOR MYSELF...

AND REMEMBER, JUST
BECAUSE IT'S NOT FUNNY

I AM NOT NORMALLY A CRUEL OR VINDICTIVE PERSON BUT I'LL MAKE AN EXCEPTION IN YOUR CASE!!!!

...AND SOMETIMES I THINK SO QUICKLY THAT MOST PEOPLE DON'T REALIZE THAT I AM THINKING AT ALL

CONFESSIONS OF A SECRET THINKER

THE SECRET HISTORY OF MODERN ART

Chapter I: The Plot is Hatched

Our story begins with Gustave Courbet
Who was a Communard by the way
He knew just which painterly button to push
A slap in the face with a fat girl's bush
And it's goodbye, Boldini, Bougereau,
Winterhalter, James Tissot,
Adieu, my poor Meissonier[1],
The Last of the Masters have had their day
And the War Against Beauty was underway

It's a muddy road to Paul Cézanne
If you like awkward, Paul's your man
Inedible apples, unbeddable nudes
Nature in one of her nastier moods
If a carpenter made a table like that
He'd be out of a job in ten seconds flat
Your school friend, Zola, thought you'd gone mad[2]
But you made it okay to paint real bad
And that was your part in the anti-art plan

So let's catch up with Vincent Van Gogh's
Provençal idyll with Paul Gauguin
Then that field of corn, those terrible crows
In the sullen glare of a clouded sun
Take that yellow chair and lend me an ear
Madness has entered the picture here
And Modernism has truly begun

George Seurat's stuff looks placid at first
But he's painting a world just going to burst
Ahead lie Bridget Riley and Op
And the spots epidemic of Damien Hirst
To say nothing of Stephen Sondheim's slop
They applaud Seurat as a pointilliste
Did you know he was also an anarchist?
Those particle clusters were only the start
Of a negative force-field too strong to resist
That would tear apart beauty and art

Pablo Picasso, a giant among men,
Said he painted like Raphael when he was ten
Came La Vie en Rose, then his whole world blued
Did someone say kitsch? That's really quite rude!
Witchdoctors to the rescue! Picasso plunged on
To 'Les Demoiselles d'Avignon'
Catch a whiff of the girls' Barcelona pong!
He hid it away. Sadly, not for long
Then he and Braque sliced and diced and glued
Some called it "Cubism" which sounded crude[3]
So as isms go it was quite a good fit

But Matisse couldn't make heads or tails of it[4]
Luxe, calme et volupté
That was Henri's way and Henri would say
That a businessman after a long hard day
Should treat his work like an easy chair
While Pablo tried styles like a man possessed
And as if in some eerie way he guessed
The needs, and the greed, the hungers he'd feed
Of collectors to come, a predator breed
It was Picasso wheeled out the shopping cart
And created the Supermarket of Art

Picasso, Modernism's first deity,
Kissed the girls and made them cry
But when Gary Cooper and Chaplin dropped by
His English embarrassed him, and that's
Why he pulled silly faces and wore silly hats
It was David Douglas Duncan's pix
In *Life* that cured his celebrity fix[5]
When Picasso grew old, this giant amongst men
Didn't paint like Raphael but a child of ten

Raymond and Jacques really painted quite well
Better by miles than their brother Marcel
But it's Marcel who's the toast of the crème de la crème.
While Raymond and Jacques have dropped out of the frame
They're goner than gone, buster than bust
While Pablo is eating Marcel's dust
Do you want to know the reason for this?
Forget Francis Naumann's analysis
Those painful puns, LHOOQ,
Make people feel cool, like nobody's fool
Marcel was a master at taking the piss!

Cocteau said the trick to being a star
Is knowing just how far to go too far
Now the Picassoid garden has long gone to seed
While Duchamp Inc. makes much of product we need
So anyone can be a belle at the art world ball
With one half-smart idea, a huge helping of gall
And no visible art-making talent at all. ◘

1. Meissonier was actually the richest artist of his time
2. Clear from reading Zola's *The Masterpiece*
3. Louis Vauxcelles, who came up with the phrase "Les Fauves" in 1905, employed the word "cubism" about a Braque in 1908. He meant it appreciatively in neither case.
4. A remark to Michel Georges-Michel, quoted in *From Renoir to Picasso*.
5. Told me by John Richardson

TO BE CONTINUED WITH CHAPTER II, THE PLOT SICKENS

SOLILOQUY IN THE TATE TURBINE HALL

A Brilliant but Inexplicably Underappreciated Artist
Contemplates Some Figures in the Landscape. Grrr!

No! I am not envious of Damien Hirst
Absolutely utterly not
Not one smidgen, one tittle, one jot
Why should I care that he's hotter than hot?
Not one iota, no thought is remoter
Do you hear me, Nick Serota?
Just because Hirst always has to be first
Because he needs to blow up or burst
Why would I want to see him immersed
In formaldehyde next to his putrid shark
And sold as a set to an oligarch?
Let's whack that idea clean out of the park!
I am NOT AT ALL jealous of Damien Hirst

I'm in Burlington House—it's a subject switch—
For some art world chowdown, I forget just which,
When out in the courtyard there's a furore
I trot outside to see what's the story
There's paparazzi, it must be a star
Posh and Becks by the brouhaha
No, it's Tracey Emin, with her bum on a car
I am not envious of Tracey Emin
She's a drama queen, who knows where she's been?
But a word in your ear, Tracey, my dear,
Whingeing won't make you Van Gogh or Soutine

Which brings us right up to the Chapman Twins
Grafting sex parts onto mannequins
In a hellish world of paranoia
They're looney bins, the Chapman Twins
Francisco Goya, call your lawyer
Some of your art died for their sins
But I half admire the Chapman Twins

You art lovers obviously all go to Frieze
Where I hope you have all of the fun of the fair.
Art here, art there, art everywhere
Like bidding rings and conspiracies
Consultants with dubious degrees
And lovely girls pimping galleries
Cutting edge? It's paper cuts
Pools of stage blood but no sign of guts
Do I go to Frieze? Are you serious? Please!
And I won't post my work on Saatchi Online
If every bad artist got slapped with a fine
It might put a stop to our culture's decline
Just calling it art doesn't mean that it's fine
So don't look for ME on Saatchi Online

If original minds, not the usual clique,
Got to put up names for the Turner Prize
You just might get a refreshing surprise
Instead of those annual sights for sore eyes
Those derivative chunks of Duchampian chic
You might see Real Art. But I fantasise
That coterie
Will never have time for the likes of ME
So they can stuff their Turner Prize
Up the appropriate part of the anatomy

So what should we make of Richard Prince?
God knows he's given us plenty of hints
The Marlbough cowboys as rephotographs
The jokes so lame that they limp in on splints
Celebrity pix with mock autographs
He's a postmodernist, a barrel of laughs,
But then something happened, Prince painted a nurse
Then nurse after nurse after nurse after nurse
The collectors pounced, the prices bounced
At which the collectors moved into reverse
They saw the fellow has been prolific
In different styles, and that was terrific
There's no product shortage like Johns or Vermeer
Picasso's the business model here
But, dear collectors, please sit on your paddles
Marlborough men, just hang up your saddles
The jokes flutter home to the Internet
Okay, I'm done. Well, not quite yet !

I forget, did I mention Damien Hirst?
I really don't want to see Damien cursed
The Lord of the Flies completely defaced
His halves of calves turn to toxic waste
His skull turned dull, his diamonds to paste
His spins come unspun, his dots all gone black
His cigarette ends stuck back in the pack
While he's teaching himself to paint in a shack
Paint like Bacon? Damien's dreaming
That sound you hear is Pope Innocent screaming! ◘

ENCOUNTER ON THE LOWER EAST SIDE

Woman
I know a genius
An undiscovered genius
I truly wish you knew this genius too

Man
Well, I know a genius
An astonishing genius
And strangely she's undiscovered too

W
He makes art from things he finds in the streets
It's so unusual the way that he thinks

M
She writes letters to interesting people she meets
She likes to use green and violet inks

W
He has inch-high tufts of facial hair
That he likes to dye with a zebra stripe
The bourgeoisie finds this hard to take
But the suits are making a bad mistake
If they think their mockery will make him break
He has no time for poseurs or hype

M
She wears sequins around her eyes
And coats from an army surplus rack
The look she achieves is completely unique
I've coined the phrase Radical Chic
She wants to blend in but although she tries
She'll never be one of the art world pack
She's got that natural, native genius
Which Jeff and Damien and Tracey lack

W
He has made a great piece out of navel fluff
It took years and years but he saved such a lot
He likes to make art out intimate stuff
Like sperm and dishonoured checks and snot
He's truly a genius, an unruly genius
Which Prince and Murakami are not

M
She's a warrior, she's no bimbo
She fights like Rambo but she writes like Rimbaud
She's finished some brilliant poetry
About beings she visits in the galaxy
It's in a language she invented, but she
Plans to include a dictionary

W
That's something I'd really like to see

M
She'll get to that eventually
(Pause)
Mine doesn't have a tattoo on his neck
Or believe that water endangers the health

W
Mine doesn't have public debates with himself
Or arrive at openings undressed for attention

M
Where she's welcome, at least. Unlike some I could mention
(They harmonise).

W & M
But we've each got a genius. An unbridled genius
Each of them a genius through and through
And you need a special instinct to recognise raw genius
So I suppose we've got a touch of genius too ◘

ART WORLD WARS

JUST *WHAT* DID YOU ASK? DO I MAKE MY ART MYSELF?

DO *I* LOOK LIKE A TOTAL LOSER?

THE GREGSONS WERE TRYING TO BUILD A DECENT CONTEMPORARY COLLECTION. BUT OUTSIDER ARTISTS KEPT BREAKING IN!!!

I MADE THIS
ART
BECAUSE I
DON'T HAVE
THE PLATES
TO PRINT
MONEY

A WORD IN YOUR EYE

HOWIE WORKS FOR A SERIOUS COLLECTOR WHO DOES NOT WISH TO BE IDENTIFIED.

FRED'S WORK HAS A LOT OF CRED IN THE HIPHOP COMMUNITY

GEORGE'S WORK IS MOVING IN AN INCREASINGLY REALIST DIRECTION.

BIGED'S WORK HAS A WRY AUTOBIOGRAPHICAL ELEMENT.

WE ALL SAW TOO LATE THAT BUD'S LAST PIECE WAS A SUICIDE NOTE

TALKING ABOUT MY GENERATION

I too have lived in Arcadia
It was paradise with an open bar
Back in that olden golden age
After the pill and before the plagues

We lit fires on several moons
Bob and the Moptops wrote our tunes
Back in that olden golden age
After the pill and before the plagues

It was a lot like Camelot
Before the grail made them lose the plot
No crack, no skunk, just wine and pot
Back in that olden golden age
After the pill and before the plagues

It was another Renaissance
But with miniskirts and bell bottom pants
Back in that olden golden age
After the pill and before the plagues

WILD CHILD

Have you heard of the wild child?
Blows into town on the wind from nowhere
Pops the eyes and sets the tongues wagging
Wakes up in her Prada, snuggled in the gutter
Tooty, toot, toot, she feels much better
Cuts off a dude's nipple with a cigar cutter
He's just a loser, she's such a cutie
Whole world's wild for the wild child

Who dares mess with this bad, bad girl?
Got a new beau, spends his money like water
Slams his hand in the door, he wasn't her fancy
Jumps out of the limo, she don't wear panties
Burns the bridge which she's still crossing
She's a reality star now, really charting
Over the top with a topless hottie
Hard to get really mad with this bad girl

Nobody wants to say no to the wild child
She sits upfront at a couture showing
Gets paid cold cash. She's bored with freebies
Now she's in a spat with a D-list starlet
Both been playing with this month's boytoy
She has to have him. She's so romantic.
He drops her like a ball of Kleenex
She says she's over being the bad girl
Tells the columns she wants a low profile
Eats bark and ginseng, really plans to read Rumi
Goes to a witch to channel Diana
She looks right at you, she isn't listening
Inside her head, people are whispering
You're a bad, bad girl, you're a mad, mad girl
But that's righty-right right. Just don't be a sad girl ◘

THE SOCIAL SCIENTIST

You've seen me around, I'm the Everywhere Man
I get out and about wherever I can
I've got an ordinary face. I wear an ordinary suit
Nobody knows me. Do I give a hoot?

When I hit the town I aim for the top
My target events are the cream of the crop
If the A-list will be at a charity hop
You'll find me difficult to stop
Benefits for the ballet, the opera, the zoo
For who cares what and who gives a shit who?

I sneak into dinners where the killer elite
Fork up a grand just to meet and greet
And to park an expensive rear end on a seat
It's that or a bag of crisps on the street

If the Clipboard Nazis start coming on hard
I can produce a business card
Which somehow seems to indicate
Although it doesn't exactly state
That I'm with a media conglomerate
So the Clipboard Nazi sometimes won't take
The risk of making a serious mistake

It's like the Clipboard Nazis came from Outer Space
To serve the PR master race
And enforce each motherfucking whim
Just to keep us lower lifeforms in our place
They aren't normal humans, they do too much gym,
But they don't often err
In telling her from her
Or him from him
So learn from me or your chances are slim

Art openings are boring, the whole world can go
Even the back office party can be cracked by a pro
If you want to hang out with Gogo & Co.
Though why you'd want that I really don't know
Posh memorials are easy, there's not often A-list
But avoid movie screenings, they're a must to be missed
You're just making up numbers for some publicist
Watching made-up stories alone in the dark
You're joking! That's not my idea of a lark

At publishers' parties there are piles of books
Pick up a couple, you may get a few looks,
But getting them signed, that's really the knack
They're worth a few quid when they go on the stack
Promotional parties in department stores
Are always a horrible sodding drag
Stuffed with bores and model stroke actress stroke whores
But fun's not the point, the point is the swag
This shirt came out of a goodie bag

But I'm not here for the goodies, the food and the drink
Nor for the pussy, I know how you think,
Why should I hit on a party girl
When I 'm a one-man gangbang of the social whirl?
So I can be chucked out now and then
By a Clipboard Nazi with a poison pen
But I'm the Everywhere Man. I know this town
And one way or another I'll bring you all down ◘

A GOOD LIFE

It's okay to get off
To a leisurely start
Behave like a toff
But a toff with a heart

You're quite the team player
You ask for advice
Say I don't want my whole share
Just a small slice
Act like you care
Pretend to be nice
Won't you please take my chair?
Thank everyone twice

Keep your slick tricks
For the third act
Then max the mix
Stack that pack

Don should take the credit
I really insist
The project got shredded?
Old Don will be missed

Those glittering frontrunners
With their brilliant careers
Don't be cruel and make fun as
They drift to the rear ◘

BLISS

A man and a woman sit at a restaurant table
He studies the menu but he'll order his usual
She'll have the cobb salad with low-cal dressing

When did it come to this?
What happened to the kissing?
Their wedded bedded bliss
What is it we are missing?

The man and the woman eat without speaking
Two store dummies dressed in the height of fashion
Two stone heads staring at the ocean

Why did it come to this?
Passion turned to ashes
What is it we are missing?

Two book-ends. But nothing that's worth reading
Two empty taxis, their meters ticking
Two old wounds that won't stop bleeding
She toys with the melon, he slices the pudding

How did it come to this?
Why aren't they reminiscing?
What is it we are missing?

Two cold fish in a poisoned river
Two dust devils whirling forever
Two loaded handguns pointing at each other
Two blank screens. The program's over.

So it has come to this
Oh, how they would kiss!
Two snakes are hissing
What is it we are missing? ◘

AN ORDINARY DAY

It's just an ordinary day
Just a day like any other
Lily's in a mood at breakfast
Snapping at her younger brother
Daddy sighs and puts the news on
The Middle East, the Middle West
For Pete's sake, Jason, get your shoes on!
Mom feels a tiny bit depressed
She flips the pages of a tabloid
Another star is in rehab
It's tragic that she's such a nutjob!
It's just an ordinary day
Just a day like any other

Daddy's stuck in morning traffic
Five cop cars race past, sirens screaming
A model smiles down from a billboard
Three more cop cars. Daddy's dreaming
She's so luscious he could touch her
Pink and precious, undies gleaming
Dangerous dad, the secret lover
The unglued traffic lurches forwards
It's just an ordinary day
Just a day like any other

Lily prances off to ballet
Mom worries so about her daughter
I know that girl is up to something!
The market's out of drinking water
Mom plans a casserole for dinner
It's really not a lot of bother!
It's just an ordinary day
Just a day like any other

Daddy's working on a big deal
It's taking months to put together
The systems all have crashed but he'll
Quite soon be ready to deliver
He thinks that it may be a winner
It's just an ordinary day
Just a day like any other

Jason's doodling at his desk
He wants to make science fiction movies
Lily gets her test results in
She calls her boyfriend but the line's down
How can she break it to her mother?
It's just an ordinary day
Just a day like any other

The radio's playing in the kitchen
These red alerts make mom quite nervous
She sniffs the bubbling casserole
And carefully puts back the cover
It's just an ordinary day
Just a day like any other
Dad climbs into his Chevrolet
He's glad the day is almost over
The day is very nearly over. ◘

SIGNS OF INTELLIGENT LIFE

THE CAVIAR GOES FIRST...
THEN THE SMOKED SALMON.

THE SCUM
ALSO RISES

DON'T FEEL YOU HAVE TO SAY IT
...JUST BECAUSE IT'S SO
TRUE!

THERE'S NO SUCH
THING AS A
"GLASS OF WINE"

HE DOESN'T KNOW HOW BORING HE IS. MAYBE YOU DON'T KNOW HOW BORING YOU ARE !

HAVE YOU NOTICED THAT HARDLY ANYBODY SAYS "BLOODY" ANYMORE?

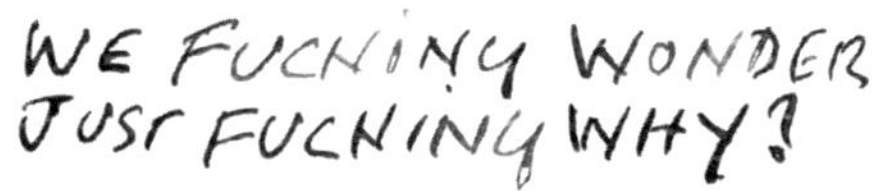

IF NOBODY SEES
YOU EAT IT...
IT ISN'T
FATTENING

IT'S OKAY TO BE A
DIRTY OLD MAN BUT
NOT A NEEDY OLD MAN

REMEMBER!

IT'S NOT HOW YOU FEEL
IT'S HOW YOU LOOK!!!

GRUESOME GEORGE

GEORGE IS APPRECIATIVE

GEORGE SYMPATHISES

GEORGE CHEERS UP A HEAVYSET PERSON

GEORGE & HANNAH AGREE

GEORGE CONSOLES A YOUNG PERSON INSECURE ABOUT HER APPEARANCE.

HARD—HEARTED HANNAH

DON'T YOU JUST WONDER HOW IN THE WORLD THEY CAME UP WITH THIS SEATING PLAN?

NO! NOT REALLY? THAT IS SO HILARIOUS
IT WAS A JOKE?

SOMETIMES I FEAR THAT I AM NO LONGER "WITH IT"
NOBODY HAS SAID "WITH IT" FOR 40 YEARS

FOR HEAVENS SAKE, ED! NOT FLOWERS THEY'RE SUCH A NUISANCE WHEN THEY DIE

SO GLAD YOU MADE THE PARTY. NOTHING WOULD HAVE BROUGHT ME OUT IN THIS WEATHER

I REALLY REALLY REALLY LIKE YOU ANNABELLE
WHY SHOULD I CARE WHAT EVERYBODY IS SAYING ABOUT YOU?

HAVEN'T I SEEN YOU SOMEWHERE?
YES. THAT'S WHY I DON'T GO THERE ANYMORE

OF COURSE I HAVE FEELINGS, BOB
CONTEMPT IS A FEELING

THE BUSINESS CYCLE

YOU'RE MY OLDEST FRIEND, ED.
I'D LIKE LIKE TO TELL YOU ABOUT
MY FINANCIAL SITUATION

UH, OKAY
LET'S
HAVE
LUNCH

WE ARE
HAVING
LUNCH,
ED

COPING WITH TOUGH TIMES

FOUR DAY STUBBLE
IS NOT A CHIC LOOK
RIGHT NOW

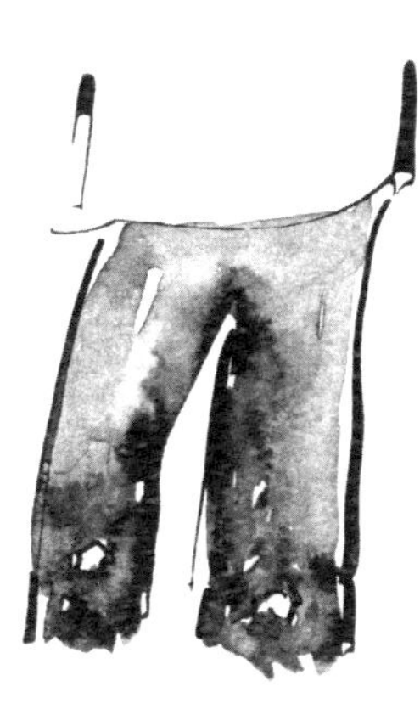

PRE-TORN JEANS
ARE NOT A GOOD LOOK

I'VE BEEN BROKE
SO LONG THAT I AM
NOW OFFICIALLY
POOR

IT DOESNT COUNT IF...

ONLY ONE OF YOU REMEMBERS IT.

IT'S A CRY FOR HELP

... IF NEITHER OF YOU KNOWS WHO THE OTHER IS!

IT WAS ONLY A MISSION of MERCY

IT'S AN ACT
OF HOMAGE

...YOU GOT A NICE
PIECE OF ART

NOW... JUST WHERE
CAN SHE HAVE HIDDEN
THAT MICROCHIP?

IT'S A MATTER
OF NATIONAL
SECURITY

...IT'S IN AUGUST!

YOU ARE ABSOLUTELY
AT ONE WITH THE COSMOS

...YOU WERE JUST
CLOWNING AROUND!!

...IT'S RESEARCH FOR
A BOOK

...YOU'RE THINKING
OF SOMEBODY ELSE

YOU TAKE THE BRATS!
GET 'EM OUT OF HERE
I QUICKLY SAW THAT THIS WAS NOT A RUN OF THE MILL CUSTODY CASE

OF COURSE I'M INVITED. MAYBE NOT SPECIFICALLY TO THIS.

SHE SAYS SHE'S CLINICALLY DEPRESSED. I SAY SHE'S PREENING

JUST BECAUSE I DON'T UNDERSTAND IT DOESN'T MEAN THAT IT'S CLEVER

MY HEART GOES OUT TO YOU FRED. THE REST OF ME IS ON HOLD

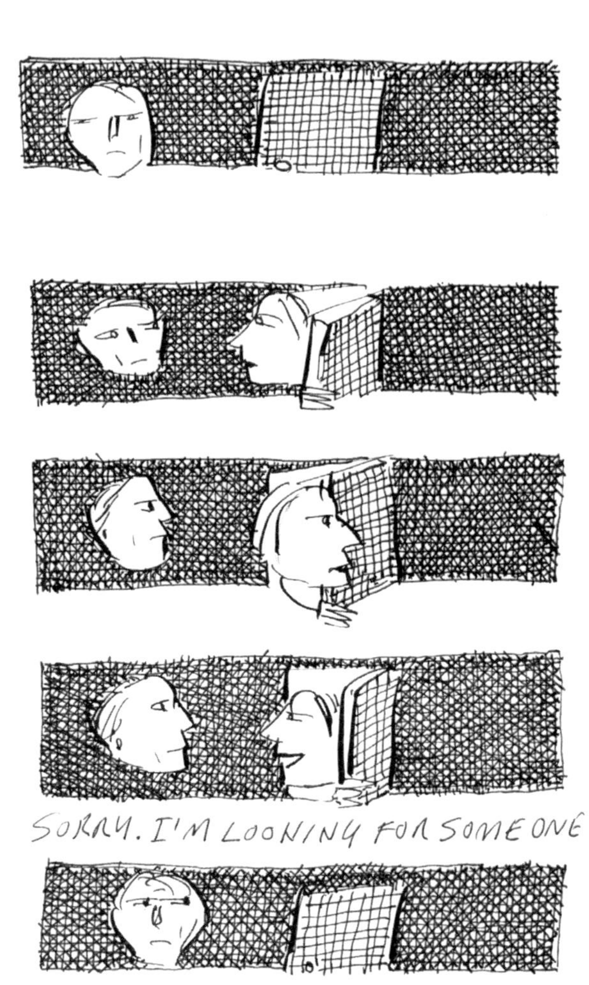
SORRY. I'M LOOKING FOR SOMEONE

I AM SOMEONE

BEN WAS REALISING THAT RESEARCHING HIS MEMOIRS WAS GOING TO BE HARDER THAN HE THOUGHT

WE LOVE SOPHIE. SHE'S
SO PETITE! PARTICULARLY
MORALLY

THE HUMAN RACE: WINNERS + LOSERS

JANE KNOWS THAT IF SHE PEERS INTO HER SMARTPHONE HARD ENOUGH SHE WILL FIND SOMEBODY WHO REALLY CARES, A DIET THAT REALLY WORKS AND THE SECRET OF ETERNAL YOUTH.

BEN SPEAKS VERY LOUDLY IN ALL PUBLIC PLACES BECAUSE HE KNOWS HE IS VERY INTERESTING AND HIS FRIEND IS ALWAYS TOO FAR AWAY!

BAD SHOES BLUES

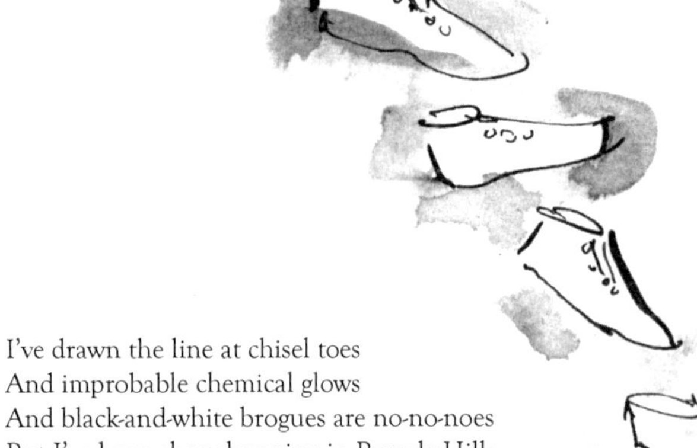

Sing the bad shoes blues.
It was an offer I couldn't refuse
Nothing but my self respect to lose
Now I've got the bad shoes blues

This song's not for twats
They know what's what
And just what goes
With their Manolos
And Jimmy Choos
This is for guys
Who aren't too wise
Whose eyes are on snooze
When they choose their shoes
Who've got the bad shoes blues

I've drawn the line at chisel toes
And improbable chemical glows
And black-and-white brogues are no-no-noes
But I've been shoe-shopping in Beverly Hills
Where I bought some bright red espadrilles
Long time ago in San Antonio
Tony Lama was the place to go
I bought some cowboy boots, black vinyl, bright
For that special occasion, a society night
Which just might end in a fight
A Mount Lebanon warlord, Christian, not Druze,
Gave me a pair of his very own shoes
Soft peanut leather and an excellent fit
But I took off the tassels and they still weren't it
I've got trainers of extreme design
An ultra aerodynamic line
So perfectly right
If I was planning to run at the speed of light
Otherwise there's little excuse
It's just the bad shoes blues

Do I hear heels clicking? Are they coming my way?
Is that a clip-clip-clopping on a nearby highway?
Is that a tap-tap-tapping up in the sky?
Sounds like they'll be here by and by
Sounds to me just like good shoes
Shoes that'll take me wherever I choose
So I can stop singing the bad shoes blues

LAST EXIT PAST GIN LANE

CRACKABYE LADY
PASSED OUT ON THE COT

ON THE BORDERLINE

YOU WILL BE STABBED!

... but WITH A SPOON
AND YOU WILL SURVIVE

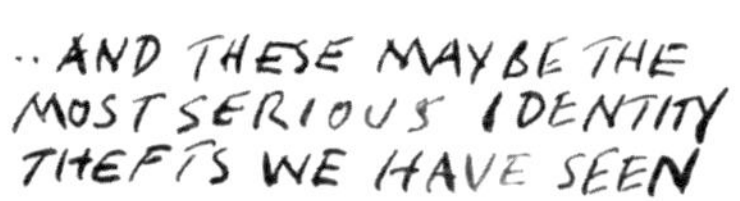

BUT UNFORTUNATELY BEPPO WAS NOT WRITING SHAKESPEARE

WATCH OUT, CAPTAIN INDESTRUCTIBLE!
THAT'S PLATINUM GIRL. HER
SUPER POWER IS SHOPPING

THOTH, THE IBIS-HEADED EGYPTIAN
MOON GOD, HAS FOR SOME REASON
SEIZED CONTROL OF YOUR MOBILE PHONE

THIS CALL
MAY BE
RECORDED
FOR YOUR
PROTECTION

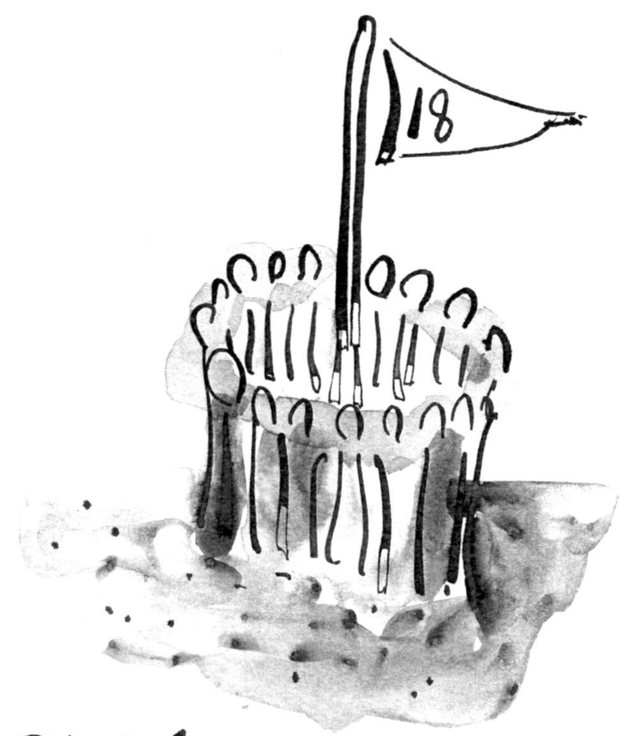

THERE'S AN APPEARANCE
OF A WHOLLY NEW SORT
OF CROP CIRCLE AT A
GOLF COURSE IN ARIZONA

THE LAST STONE

RUDELY
INTERRUPTED

FINALLY!
BEYOND
IRONY

BUT WHAT
ABOUT MY
UNFINISHED
BUSINESS?

SO!
I WAS
WRONG

I WAS
HOPING
TO GO
HOME

MY PARTY

Who's come to my party
Down on the beach?
Scarlett O'Hara
Tristan Tzara
And Jimmy Carter
Who drank sparkling water
Lollo Ferrari
Harry Houdini
Francis Picabia
The Dalai Lama
The girls of St Trinian's
Arthur Craven
Bela Lugosi
Limping Lord Byon
Akiro Kurosawa
I saw several Gettys
Getting looped on Frascati
Anna Pavlova
Lotte Lenya
The Silver Surfer
Peter Lorre
Laurel + Hardy
Krazy and Ignatz
Miuccia Prada
Salvador Dali
And the Flying Wallendas
John Cale and Ry Cooder
Saki and Taki
There goes the Glenfiddich!
Saint Frida Kahlo
Kiri te Kanawa,
John McCracken,
Truman Capote,
And The Illuminati
Getting flighty and naughty
More cocktails for each!
Now let's start partying
Down on the beach!

Who's persona non grata
Down on the beach?
Who's banned from the party?
Who's not on the list?
Paris Hilton,
Any Tea Party
Except the Mad Hatter's
Professor Moriarty
Anybody called Simon
Except Simon de Pury
Mark "Scratchy" Thatcher
Aleister Crowley
Peter Fallow
Silvio Berlusconi
Nicolas Sarkozy
L. Ron Hubbard
Liberace
Donatella Versace,
Fundamentalists
With TV ministries
Media twisters
With ugly histories
Columnists
With lying bylines
And lilac eyeliner
Who kiss and diss.
But you promised and promised
I'd be on the list!
You won't be missed
You're hardly martyrs
You're just masochists
It's hard to resist
Being a bit of a tartar
Down on the beach

What is this vision?
From over the sea?
A giant white yacht, she hits the spot

A bright apparition, a nifty addition
She's a humdinger, a lulu, a peach
She's every possible figure of speech
But what perplexes us down on the beach
Is why did they come here? Who can they be?

Vanity Fair's taking photographs
Down on the sand
They've found a power couple
He's plump and she's supple
They're having loads of laughs
He's fondling her hand
She's flashing a nipple
He has an old face
She has a cold face
But they'll get into bold face
Perhaps a whole paragraph
So we quite understand

The white ship is floating
Like a gull on the bay
There's dancing on deck. We hear music play.
We're sure we've been spotted
They'll be coming to join us
Quite soon they'll be coming
In glimmering white dinghies
They'll dance at our party
Then they'll take us away

Now comes the sunset
Down on the beach
It's hilariously trashy
All greens, golds and purples
That turn the sand ashen
The beach is a funfair
Extraordinary fireworks
Whoosh right above us
Day-bright above us
Until the sky blackens
So now my party
Has really got started
We don't mean to slacken
Which is when we get startled
Down on the beach

The white yacht is departing
It sails out of reach
Beyond the horizon
We're wholly dumbfounded
We're really down-hearted
No dinghies are coming
We're stuck at my party
Down on the beach.

The Beautiful People
Start drifting off early.
The men on the gate are sullen and useless
The barmen move slowly, the waiters are surly
The beautiful hatcheck is sad-eyed and listless
It's quite a fiasco
Down on the beach.

What a dire Morning After
Down on the beach
An ugly aftermath
I hear harsh laughter
And hacking coughing
Rustling in the dune grass
Some lie inertly
Each next to each
It's a masterclass for sociopaths
I'm done with roving
There'll be no more loving
There'll be no more parties
Ever or ever
Down on the beach

WELCOME TO THE HOTEL SUPER—EUROPE

Welcome to the Hotel Super-Europe
We were true believers
It seemed to take forever
But now it's a dream achieved
A hotel fit for heroes
If you've got the euros
We'll be the survivors
Mein gott! Magnifico! My goodness! We are so relieved!

Machiavelli is our concierge in the Hotel Super-Europe
He knows what's what, where's where and who's who
Other hotel empires
Lack our kind of pizzaz
Take the Hotel US,
Tradition isn't something that they do
You see we wrote the books and made the pictures too

We have swell events in the ballroom of the Hotel Super-Europe
Yes, we're wined and we're dined
But you'll be certain to find
That famine and drought are much on our mind
We're so haunted by AIDS and the disease of the week
As we dance chic to chic
Elsewhere hotels may be going to hell
But we're doing good and we're doing well
That's how we do things in the Hotel Super-Europe

You'll love the Watteau Gardens at the Hotel Super-Europe
We have lakes, swings, gazebos and conservatories too
Other hotel gardens are being lost
To desert, swamp and permafrost
But we still act the perfect host
Serve wine and cheese and offer quite a view
That is, at least, to a discerning few
We try to keep up standards in the Hotel Super-Europe

You can use the Siegfried health club in the Hotel Super-Europe
A spa with rubber mats and smart machines
Phew! How we sweat at melting off those grams
And toning up our bums. tums, abs and hams
We come from condottieri, conquistadores, kings and queens
It's something coded in our warrior genes

There'll be no morning paper in the Hotel Super-Europe
Opinions divide folks, don't you agree?
Because you see
Social Democracy
Is so Twentieth Century
And we prefer authority
In the simpatico hands of celebrity
That's why it's all good news in the Hotel Super-Europe

There's been a kitchen revolution in the Hotel Super-Europe
Chef Anatole don't work here anymore
We've got a Brit who talks more blue than you know who
And a Spaniard who turns fish to foam and steak to glue
That's our creative cuisine in the Hotel Super-Europe
And there's always a fast burger joint next door

You'll love the Kafka Gift Shop in the Hotel Super-Europe
We, after all, invented souvenirs
Witty cushions, cultured carrier bags.
T-shirts on which invention never sags
Underpants bright with patriotic flags
Sam Beckett is in charge of publications,
The postcard racks, the neatly framed quotations
From business leaders of our member nations
And complete sets of EU regulations
There's stuff enough to have fun with for years
And I think you may be sometimes moved to tears
You won't leave empty-handed from the Hotel Super-Europe

You'll bop in the Disco Darwin in the Hotel Super-Europe
Charlemagne and Dicky Lionheart play the hits
From North Africa, the Caribbean and the Congo
And other places we have loved to bits

We're proud of our room service in the Hotel Super-Europe
Our trolleys slide down quiet corridors
Bringing great food and drink to the right doors
Perhaps not yours or yours or yours or yours or yours
We do see that it's troubling
That the population's doubling
And regret there will be difficulties to come.
For some.
Are those corks popping at the outer gate?
We haven't had that vintage here since 1968
We're absolutely not predicting doom.
But there've been changes at the Hotel Super-Europe
Room service can no longer offer room ◘

The *Ballade des dames de temps jadis*, the *Ballad of the Ladies of Times Past*, was written by Francois Villon, a 15th-century French poet, described by Wikipedia as a "poet, thief and vagabond." It became famous for its refrain '*Mais ou sont les neiges d'antan?*' which was translated by Dante Gabriel Rossetti as '*Where are the snows of yesteryear?*' It is itself a bit faded now, appropriately enough, but it was quoted in Tarantino's *Inglourious Basterds*.

MAIS OU SONT LES NEIGES D'ANTAN?

Where are the snows of yesteryear?
Or hula hoops or greaser hair?
Miles or Bird blowing the Blues?
The Jet Set and those Panam stews?
Hot pants or the bubble dress?
The Baader Meinhof, the SDS?
Moon rocks, pet rocks, Rockets Redglare?
Italian scooters everywhere
Mood rings, love beads or Condomania
Sonny and Cher to entertain you
Could you dish up nouvelle cuisine?
Master a new pinball machine?
Can you do the Frug? The Jerk? The Twist?
Were you on Liz or Suzy's list?
But that I think is quite enough
Of rootling through this thrift store stuff
Forget the easy memorabilia
I want to thrill you, chill you, kill you
So follow as we make the scene.

The race for the four minute mile
See the Pyramids along the Nile
Audrey Hepburn's spiffing style
Carmen Miranda on a tropic isle
Bobby Short at the Carlyle
Wooo! To the dark half of the dial
And this may take a little while
J. Edgar Hoover's curdled bile
Lee Harvey Oswald's bulging file
Jayne Mansfield in a speeding motor
Vic Morrow underneath a rotor
Mark Chapman outside the Dakota
Robert Maxwell does a floater
Squeaky Fromme at the Manson trial
OJ Simpson in denial
The way that Enron made their pile
Bernie Madoff's tiny smile
Mais ou sont les neiges d'antan?
We know just where those folks have gone

Where have the war reporters gone?
A bottle of Dewars, your Olivetti
Your boat is waiting at the jetty
Brash mercenaries, a chartered plane
You're off doing that dumb stuff again
Biafra, checkpoints, Lebanon
Though you're a bozo with a gun
You're an action hack, you're Superman!
Now magazines are limp and wan
There's no one calling you at dawn
Mais ou sont les neiges d'antan?

Where are the snows of yesteryear?
The joys of *La Vie Litteraire?*
What happened to the literati
Who'd flock to a George Plimpton party?
The grouchy writers at Elaine's
Beating out each other's brains?
Kurt Vonnegut and Irwin Shaw,
Norman, Truman, absent Gore?
Mais ou sont les neiges d'antan?
Where have New York's last writers gone?
Off to tenure, every one?

Mais ou sont lest neiges d'antan?
Have the photographers all gone?
Ask Henri Cartier-Bresson,
Irving Penn, Dick Avedon
Bailey, Duffy, Donovan
Helmut Newton, Guy Bourdin
Just ask who Mary Ellen Mark's
Retoucher is? Expect some sparks
Don McCullin, Jim Nachtwey
Photoshop wiped your world away
We've pixillated verité
Now phones take pictures everywhere
All that is solid melts into air
Where are the snows of yesteryear?

Where are the babes of times gone by?
Chin chin, pudding! Here's mud in your eye!
Make yourself comfy, sweetypie!
Stunning dress, honey! Wouldn't it look even more
Stunning, lying on my bedroom floor?
That always got the room in a roar
The cinq a sept, the roll in the hay
The cow's away, please won't you stay?
Hiding the salami, fun games to play
Mais ou sont les dames du temps jadis?
And do they still remember me?

Okay! Now we're in Italy.
La Dolce Vita, the Veneto
An MGM starlet in a palazzo
The paparazzi on the go-go-go
Scandals erupt in *Il Specchio!*
But suddenly it's Roma Addio
Mais ou sont les neiges d'antan?
Where have the playboy princes gone?

So it's off to London Babylon
Where we have reinvented fun
No more war but lots more pot
A rich girl in a Fulham squat
Peter Sellers and Sophia
In Alvaro's trattoria
Michael Caine and Terence Stamp
Dine at Annabel's, dance at Tramp
Art and fashion both go Pop
While the last of the empire is going under
Keith Moon, Syd Barrett and Brian Jones
No more rolling for that Stone
Have all the Birds of Britain flown?
What of soul was left, I wonder,
When the swinging had to stop?

Ciao, Manhattan! We're Eurotrash
You need class and we need cash
Late afternoons in Fiorucci
Plato's Retreat for hootchie-cootchie
Mortimers and Jackie O
El Morocco, Studio
The VIP room waits below
What happened to *that* snow we know

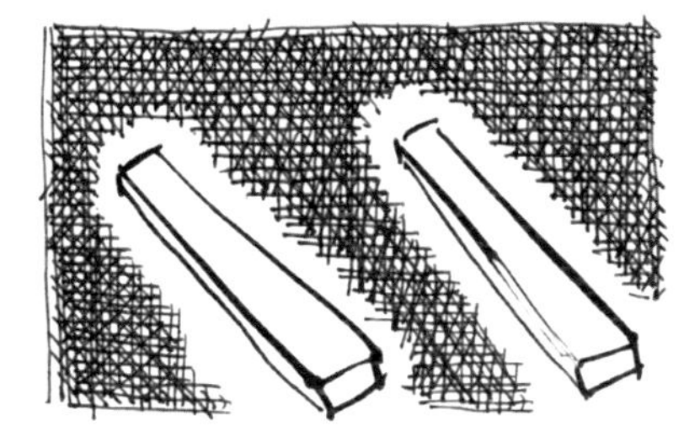

Through the drifting snows of memory
Twin Towers appear in front of me
The Twin Towers not of Tolkien
But Twin Towers built for businessmen
In their time on earth too big, too dumb
Just skyline hogs on the waterfront
Perfect for Philippe Petit's stunt
Then they were blown to Kingdom Come
By death and grief and fear defined
Two perfect forms, Hope and Despair,
Float suspended in the mind
Glimmering in our darkening air

So it's back to you, Francois Villon,
Poet, thief, vagabond and *con*
It's fine to sigh for *les neiges d'antan*
But what we'd really like to know
Is will we see tomorrow's snow?
And will there be tomorrow's snow? ◘